I Want to Be a
BRACHIOSAURUS

by Thomas Kingsley Troupe

illustrated by Jomike Tejido

PICTURE WINDOW BOOKS

a capstone imprint

"Brock!" my best friend Zach shouted. "Come chase us!"
I jumped for the monkey bars, but I couldn't reach them.
All of the other kids were taller.

"Hurry, Brock!" another kid shouted. "We're getting away!"

"I want to be a Brachiosaurus," I whispered. "Then I'd be taller than everyone!"

The next thing I knew, I turned into a Brachiosaurus!
It was amazing! With my head towering over the playground,
I could see far into the distance.

Every step I took made the ground tremble. I hoped
I wouldn't cause an earthquake.

My school and the playground faded away. I saw tall, strange trees in their place. Smaller dinosaurs ran through fields of ferns. Strange plants grew everywhere.

The air was heavy and hot. I ducked my head as a flying lizard screeched by.

AERO-DINO-MIC! More than 130 types of Pterosaurs lived in prehistoric times. Some of these flying reptiles were as small as a sparrow. Others were as big as a single-engine airplane!

5

My body was huge! I was as tall as my dad's four-story office building. My front legs were longer than my back legs. They felt like giant tree trunks.

My skin was thick and tough like leather. And I had a tail! It was like having a powerful arm behind me.

I met two other Brachiosaurs. Their names were Stretch and Clompy.

"Hey, buddy," Stretch said. "You look lost."

"Want to join our herd?" Clompy asked. I didn't see any other dinosaurs around. I guess they were talking to me!

"Okay, sure," I said.

"Good," Clompy said with a big smile. "It's nice to have friends."

I was getting hungry and felt like eating a salad. That was a first! "You look hungry. We know where there are lots of trees," Stretch said. He and Clompy led the way.

The nostrils on top of my tiny head perked up. I could smell those delicious leaves!

A group of dinosaurs that looked like small Tyrannosaurus rexes ran at us. They had giant heads full of sharp teeth.

"These Torvosaurs never learn," Clompy said. She swung her tail and knocked two off their feet. The others ran at me. I stomped my front feet and the ground shook.

All of them ran off. We were too big to mess with!

TONS OF FUN! Brachiosaurus was six times heavier than an elephant. That's around 33 tons (30 metric tons)! No wonder Brachiosaurs had very few predators!

"Nice work back there," Stretch said. "Now let's eat."

As a kid I never really liked salads, but my big dino stomach was rumbling. I got close to what looked like a pine tree and took a giant bite. My big, flat teeth stripped the branches bare.

"Delicious," Stretch said.

"It is," I said and chomped another mouthful. "But it kind of pokes the inside of my mouth!"

"There are small, leafier plants down lower," Clompy said. "But you don't get as much to eat."

I got used to eating from the needle trees. I was lucky and found a palm tree too. I felt like I ate about 100 pounds worth of tree!

The three of us moved on. We had eaten almost all of the branches and leaves.

"We'll be hungry again before you know it," Clompy said.

WANT A SALAD WITH THAT SALAD? Researchers estimate that Brachiosaurus ate between 200 and 800 pounds (91 and 363 kilograms) of plants every day!

Up ahead I saw a Brachiosaurus lay an egg. The egg plopped into a small hole in the ground that held a few more eggs. A moment later the mama turned around and began pushing dirt into the hole.

"Wow!" I said. "Is she going to bury those eggs?"

"That's how she'll keep them safe," Stretch said.

YOU'RE GROUNDED! Mama Brachiosaurs buried their eggs in small nests, much like sea turtles do today.

Nearby, a spot on the ground seemed to move. A few minutes later, a baby Brachiosaurus poked its head out of the dirt. I watched as it dug its way out. It was little, about the size of an adult house cat!

The mom looked at the baby and walked off, leaving it alone.

"Hey, where's the mama going?" I asked. The little Brachiosaurus looked confused.

"Her job is done," Clompy said. "When you're a dinosaur, you figure out life on your own."

She was right. The little dinosaur went after a small, leafy plant and tore it to shreds.

We left the nesting grounds behind.

Stretch looked ahead and got excited. "Our kind like to travel in herds," he said. "Maybe we should join those guys up there!"

Up ahead there were four older Brachiosaurs and a few younger ones. We moved quickly to catch up with them.

I noticed the young ones kept to the middle of the group.

As we got close, Clompy nodded toward the distance. "We've got company!"

Three Allosaurs ran toward us. One of them tried to nab a baby Brachiosaurus. Our herd closed up the circle to protect the young ones.

One member of the herd used its tail to knock down an Allosaurus. Another looked like he was about to stomp on its head.

The two remaining Allosaurs ran off, leaving their defeated friend behind.

"Whoa," I said. "Don't mess with these plant eaters!"

We stuck with the herd, which made me feel safe. We were the biggest dinosaurs around. We didn't need to have sharp, scary teeth.

Our herd moved past an older-looking Brachiosaurus. He was having trouble lifting his head.

"Hey, Clompy," I asked. "How old is that one?"

"Oh, I'd say Wrinkles is close to 90 years old. Maybe a little more," she said.

THE BIGGER AND SLOWER THEY ARE, THE LONGER THEY . . . LIVE?
The life span of a Brachiosaurus was about 100 years. Bigger and slower animals have longer life spans. A great example is the giant tortoise. Some live more than 200 years.

We stopped for a break and I looked around. I tried to figure out where in the world we were. I saw large mountains in the distance.

Were we in North America? I couldn't imagine big beasts like us roaming around the places where people live now.

DINO DISCOVERY
In 1903 paleontologist Elmer Riggs found the first Brachiosaurus skeleton in Colorado. Six years later another man found Brachiosaurus fossils in Tanzania, Africa.

Colorado

Tanzania

As we walked along, I noticed the bare trees. They were eaten by herds of roaming salad eaters.

"We're going to run out of food," I said.

"There's plenty," Stretch said. "What's the worst that could happen?"

I looked to the sky and saw a bunch of meteors heading toward the earth. Before I could even panic, I heard a loud ringing noise.

MASS EXTINCTION MYSTERY! Scientists don't know for sure how dinosaurs became extinct. Meteorite strikes and volcanic eruptions may have been to blame. Ash and dust from these events would have blocked out sunlight. Without sunlight, the plants dinosaurs needed to survive would have died.

"The recess bell," I whispered. And before I knew it, I changed back into a boy. The world changed back too.

I gripped the monkey bars. I had reached them! Some of my friends cheered for me until the bell rang again. I dropped from the monkey bars and ran toward school.

"How'd you reach those bars, Brock?" Zach asked.

I pushed out my neck as high as it would go, then shrugged. "Just had to stretch a bit, I guess."

While I was happy to be myself again, I sure was going to miss the view as a Brachiosaurus!

MORE ABOUT BRACHIOSAURUS

Brachiosaurus lived in the late Jurassic Period, more than 145 million years ago.

Brachiosaurus had a small head and chisel-like teeth. It had a big nose with nostrils down on its snout. The big nose may have been important for more than just smelling. It also may have helped cool the dinosaur's blood.

Because Brachiosaurus was so tall, it could eat the leaves on trees and plants other plant-eating dinosaurs couldn't reach.

Brachiosaurus means "arm lizard." It was given its name because of its long front legs, or "arms."

Adult Brachiosaurs had few predators. But young Brachiosaurs had to battle meat eaters such as Allosaurs and Torvosaurs.

Scientists think baby Brachiosaurs grew to the size of their parents in about 20 to 30 years.

GLOSSARY

extinct—no longer living; an extinct animal is one that has died out, with no more of its kind

fossil—the remains or traces of an animal or a plant, preserved as rock

herd—a large group of animals that lives or moves together

life span—the number of years a certain kind of plant or animal usually lives

meteor—a piece of rock or dust that enters Earth's atmosphere, causing a streak of light in the sky

meteorite—a piece of meteor that falls all the way to the ground

nostrils—openings in the nose used to breathe and smell

paleontologist—a scientist who studies fossils

predator—an animal that hunts other animals for food

prehistoric—from a time before history was recorded

READ MORE

Gregory, Josh. *Brachiosaurus*. Dinosaurs. Ann Arbor, Mich.: Cherry Lake Publishing, 2016.

Holtz, Thomas R. *Digging for Brachiosaurus: A Discovery Timeline*. Dinosaur Discovery Timelines. North Mankato, Minn.: Capstone Press, 2015.

Nunn, Daniel. *Brachiosaurus*. All About Dinosaurs. Chicago: Heinemann Library, 2015.

INTERNET SITES

FactHound offers a safe, fun way to find internet sites related to this book. All of the sites on FactHound have been researched by our staff.

Here's all you do:
Visit *www.facthound.com*
Type in this code: 9781479587704

Check out projects, games and lots more at
www.capstonekids.com

INDEX

BOOKS IN THE SERIES

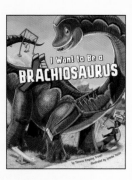
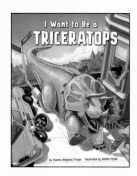
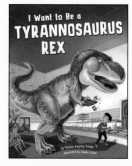
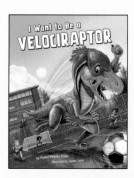

Dedication: To Travis, who always puts his neck out for others . . . like a Brachiosaurus!

Thanks to our adviser for his expertise, research, and advice:
Mathew J. Wedel, PhD
Associate Professor
Western University of Health Services

Editors: Christopher Harbo and Anna Butzer
Designer: Sarah Bennett
Art Director: Ashlee Suker
Production Specialist: Kathy McColley

The illustrations in this book were planned with pencil on paper and finished with digital paints.

Picture Window Books are published by Capstone,
1710 Roe Crest Drive, North Mankato, Minnesota 56003
www.capstonepub.com

Library of Congress Cataloging-in-Publication Data
Catalogue-in-publication information is on file with the Library of Congress.

ISBN 978-1-4795-8770-4 (library binding)
ISBN 978-1-4795-8774-2 (eBook PDF)

Summary: Follows a young boy as he transforms into a Brachiosaurus and experiences life from a dinosaur's perspective.

Printed and bound in the USA.
009685F16